Stars Shine

KINGFISHER

NEW YORK

KINGFISHER
LONDON & NEW YORK

Copyright © Kingfisher 2012
Published in the United States by Kingfisher,
175 Fifth Ave., New York, NY 10010
Kingfisher is an imprint of Macmillan Children's Books, London.
All rights reserved.

Written and designed by Dynamo Ltd.

Distributed in the U.S. and Canada by Macmillan,
175 Fifth Ave., New York, NY 10010

Library of Congress Cataloging-in-Publication data has been applied for.

ISBN 978-0-7534-7007-7

Kingfisher books are available for special promotions and premiums. For details contact:
Special Markets Department, Macmillan, 175 Fifth Ave., New York, NY 10010.

For more information, please visit www.kingfisherbooks.com

Printed in China
9 8 7 6 5 4 3 2 1
1TR/0612/HH/-/140MA

Contents

What is in space?

Our planet, Earth, is floating in space along with many other planets, stars, and moons.

A star is a giant ball of flaming gas. A planet is a world that orbits (goes around) a star. A moon is a smaller world that orbits a planet.

Out in space

- Nobody knows how big space is or how many stars and planets there are.
- People who study the stars and planets are called astronomers.
- Scientists think that space might be slowly spreading outward and getting bigger.

Earth is a planet, traveling around the Sun

The Sun is a star

The Moon goes around Earth

There are spacecraft out in space, too

5

Why do stars shine?

Stars are balls of very hot gases.

They make a lot of heat and light with their gases. We can see their light shining in the night sky and feel the heat from our closest star, the Sun.

All about stars

- Stars are not really star shaped—they are round.
- Stars only seem star shaped because of the way their light twinkles in the sky.
- Stars are not all the same size. Some stars are much bigger than the Sun, and some are much smaller.

Stars are born when dust and gas come together inside a giant space cloud

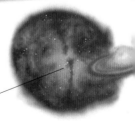

A star will
shine for many
billions of years

Toward the end of its life,
a star will swell up and
become a red giant

Eventually,
the star will
cool down

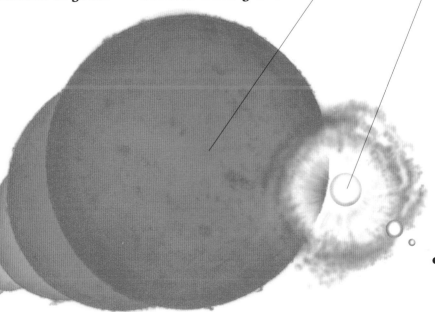

The Sun will not
cool down for another
five billion years

What is the Milky Way?

Together, a group of stars is called a galaxy. The Milky Way is the name of the galaxy that we live in.

The Sun is one of about 1,000 billion stars in the Milky Way.

The Milky Way

- The Milky Way got its name because it looks like a band of milky white light in the sky.

- There are probably about 100 billion galaxies in space.

- Galaxies are not all shaped like spirals. Some of them are shaped like eggs, and some have no special shape.

The Milky Way
is shaped like
a spiral

It looks like a
giant whirlpool

This is where
the Sun is found
in the Milky Way

9

Which planets are our neighbors?

Earth has seven neighboring planets that also orbit the Sun.

Uranus

The Sun, Earth, and its neighbors are together called the solar system.

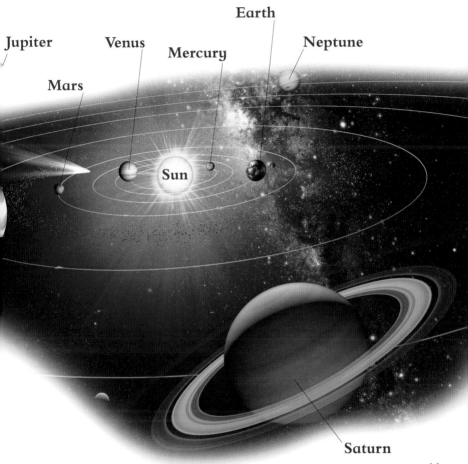

Jupiter

Mars

Venus

Mercury

Earth

Neptune

Sun

Saturn

11

Are the other planets like ours?

Earth is the only solar system planet with plants and animals on it. It gets just the right amount of heat and light from the Sun for living things to exist.

Planets that are closer to the Sun than Earth are too hot for animals and plants to live on. Planets that are farther away are too cold.

Earth and the planets

- Some solar system planets are much larger than Earth is and some are smaller.

- Mars is our closest neighboring planet. It would take about nine months to travel there in a space rocket.

- All of the planets spin as they orbit the Sun.

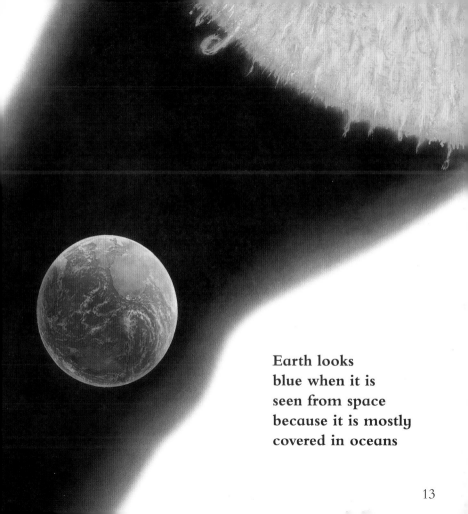

Earth looks
blue when it is
seen from space
because it is mostly
covered in oceans

Which planets are giants?

Jupiter, Saturn, Uranus, and Neptune
are all very big planets. They are
mostly made of gas, so they
are called the gas giants.

Jupiter is the largest
planet in the solar
system. It is so big
that all of the other
planets could fit
inside it.

The giant planets

- You couldn't stand on
  Jupiter, Saturn, Uranus,
  or Neptune because they
  are mostly made of gas.

- The gas would be very
  poisonous to humans.

- Jupiter looks as if it has
  beautiful swirling patterns
  on it. These are made by
  gas clouds blown around
  by superstrong winds.

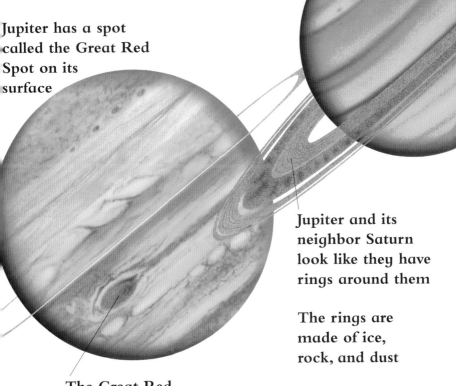

Jupiter has a spot called the Great Red Spot on its surface

Jupiter and its neighbor Saturn look like they have rings around them

The rings are made of ice, rock, and dust

The Great Red Spot is a gigantic storm raging on the planet

Which planets are supercold?

The planets that are farthest away from the Sun are the coldest. Neptune is incredibly cold, and so is Uranus.

Neptune and Uranus both get their blue color from a gas called methane. Methane smells like rotten eggs, so these planets must be very smelly, too.

The coldest planets

- Scientists have learned about the faraway planets by sending unmanned spaceships called space probes to study them.
- The space probes send photos and measurements back to Earth.
- Neptune is so far away that it took twelve years for the space probe *Voyager 2* to reach it from Earth.

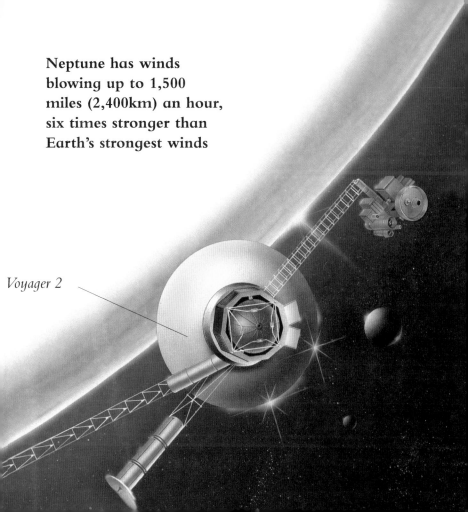

Neptune has winds blowing up to 1,500 miles (2,400km) an hour, six times stronger than Earth's strongest winds

Voyager 2

How hot is the Sun?

The Sun is superhot. It is hottest in the middle and slightly cooler on the outside. But even on the outside it is still 25 times hotter than the hottest kitchen oven.

Giant flaming sheets of glowing gas shoot out from the Sun's surface.

The Sun

- The Sun's light takes eight minutes to reach Earth.
- Earth spins around as it orbits the Sun. When your home is facing away from the Sun, you experience nighttime.
- It takes the Earth 24 hours to spin around in space and one year to orbit the Sun.

Dark patches called sunspots sometimes show up on the Sun's surface

Sunspots are places where the Sun has turned a slightly different temperature. They don't last very long.

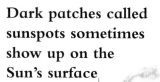

What is it like to visit space?

To get into space, astronauts must speed away from Earth onboard a rocket.

There is no air to breathe in space, and it can be very hot or very cold. Humans need space suits to protect them and an air supply to keep them alive.

Visiting a space station

- Some astronauts live onboard a space station orbiting Earth.
- They travel to and from the space station onboard rockets.
- The astronauts on the space station do science experiments and study outer space.

In 1969, American astronauts walked on the Moon for the first time

They found that the Moon was dry and rocky

What do you know about space?

You can find all of the answers to these questions in this book.

Do you know the name of the galaxy we live in?

Is the Sun a star or a moon?

Do you think the Sun is as hot as an oven, or hotter?

Can you name another planet?

Why do you think the Earth looks blue from space?

Why do astronauts have to wear space suits in space?

Would you like to visit space one day?

Some space words

Galaxy A giant group of stars.

Moon A small world that goes around a larger planet.

Orbit The path that an object takes around and around another object.

Planet A world that travels around a star. Earth is a planet.

Solar system The Sun and all the planets and moons that orbit it.

Space station A spacecraft orbiting Earth on which astronauts can live for a while.

Star A giant flaming ball of gas in space. The Sun is a star.